VITAL SIGNS

Conversing with God

J. Michael Ripski

Abingdon Press
Nashville

CONVERSING WITH GOD

Copyright © 1992 by Abingdon Press

This book is printed on recycled, acid-free paper.

Library of Congress Cataloging-in-Publication Data

Ripski, J. Michael, 1949—
    Conversing with God / J. Michael Ripski.
        p.   cm. — (Vital signs series)
    ISBN 0-687-09633-2 (alk. paper)
    1. Prayer. I. Title. II. Series.
BV210.2.R52   1992
248.3'2—dc20   91-42392
                                                                  CIP

Scripture quotations are from the New Revised Standard Version of the
Bible, copyright 1989 by the Division of Christian Education of the National
Council of Churches of Christ in the USA.

MANUFACTURED IN THE UNITED STATES OF AMERICA

To my wife, Suzanne, who, through her love, honesty, and forgiveness, has taught me much about conversation that is prayerful.

Vital Signs. What does that mean? In the context of the human body, vital signs are marks of health and life—pulse rate, blood pressure, body temperature. What might *vital signs* mean for the church?

Vital signs in the life of the Body of Christ consist of features of congregational life that define and measure its health, its vigor. Such signs include prayer, study, outreach, and worship. These signs are found on several levels. The spiritual life of each member contributes to the spirituality of the entire congregation. Group study, especially Bible study, enriches the congregation in knowledge and understanding. Outreach binds individuals in a common purpose. Worship tailored to private and corporate meditation and praise yields a sense of authentic community before God.

The Vital Signs books have been created to help the people of God register vital signs of life for service to one another and to God, who "made us alive together with Christ" (Eph. 2:5). To that end this series is dedicated.

C O N T E N T S

INTRODUCTION
A Cry for Intimacy...................................... 9
An Invitation to Honesty........................... 11
Where We Usually Begin........................... 13
A New Beginning...................................... 15

CHAPTER ONE
Prayer: Our Conversation with God...................17
God Began the Conversation.........................18
Our Response... 20
The Conversation Was Interrupted...............21
Our Corrupt Language and World.............. 23
The Conversation Is Restored.....................27
A New Language for a New World..............28

CHAPTER TWO
The Power of Prayer...................................... 31
The Power of the Holy Spirit......................32
What Shall We Pray For?...........................34

How Shall We Pray?................................ 39
Are We to Pray for Healing?....................... 41
What About Unanswered Prayer?................. 42
A Personal Experience of Answered Prayer.... 45

CHAPTER THREE
The Purposes of Prayer................................. 49
Prayer Is Adoration and Praise.................... 50
Prayer Is Confession................................. 52
Prayer Is Intercession............................... 55
Prayer Is Petition.................................... 58
Prayer Is Thanksgiving.............................. 59
Corporate Worship as Prayer...................... 61

CHAPTER FOUR
Disciplines for Prayer................................. 63
Practicing the Presence of God.................... 64
Praying the Scriptures............................... 65
Praying Through Writing........................... 66
Guided Meditation................................... 70
Praying with Others................................. 73
Corporate Intercessory Prayer.................... 75
A Word About Solitude............................. 76

CHAPTER FIVE
Transformed by Prayer................................. 79
The Prayerful Are Centered........................ 80
The Prayerful Are Patient and Persevering.... 83
The Prayerful Are Discerning...................... 85
The Prayerful Are Vital............................. 87
The Prayerful Are Hopeful......................... 89
The Prayerful Follow Jesus......................... 90

Suggested Further Reading............................. 93

Are any among you suffering? They should pray. Are any cheerful? They should sing songs of praise. Are any among you sick? They should call for the elders of the church and have them pray over them, anointing them with oil in the name of the Lord. The prayer of faith will save the sick, and the Lord will raise them up; and anyone who has committed sins will be forgiven. Therefore confess your sins to one another, and pray for one another, so that you may be healed. The prayer of the righteous is powerful and effective. (James 5:13-16)

A Cry for Intimacy

Today we hear and read a lot about intimacy. There are good reasons. In a high-tech world, there is a growing hunger for experiences that are "high touch." At almost every turn we speak and listen to computers. Machines, no matter how "smart" they are, make us feel demeaned. Aren't we important enough to receive attention from a human being?

Our technology and standard of living have permitted an increase in individual freedom, but at a price. Our right and ability to retreat to the privacy of our own homes has had the consequence of estrangement and isolation. We often feel trapped by our struggle for independence, on the one hand, and our need for intimacy, on the other.

The authors of *Habits of the Heart* observe that our family life is devoted to producing individuals with the ego strength to leave home. The family that enables its members to exist on their own is successful. Ironically, then, our basic socializing unit exists for the purpose of making us antisocial.

Recall the familiar proverb: "Train children in the right way, and when old, they will not stray" (Proverbs 22:6). If we are trained to define adulthood in terms of independence and self-sufficiency, then when we become adults we spend our lives "looking out for number one."

But looking out for number one leaves us starved for intimacy. We seek companionship—not because we are too weak to make it on our own, but because something inside us cries out to know others and to be known by them. We want to love and be loved. We can't explain it. We simply confess that this is the way we are.

This book is about intimacy. More precisely, it is about prayer, which is conversation that expresses and creates intimacy. This intimacy is with the One who created us, the One in whom we live and move and have our being. Because of this One, whose name is above all names, we are able to enjoy intimacy with others. Our intimacy with God makes genuine intimacy with others possible. Without intimacy with God, our intimacy with others is destined to be undermined and corrupted by our self-centeredness. Then what is called intimacy is nothing but a one-night stand.

Prayer enables us to break out of the bondage of our perverted individualism. Prayer helps us to see that our personal welfare cannot be viewed separately from the welfare of all, including creation.

The church has been called into being to keep the conversation going between God and God's children. The church is birthed by prayer—by God's Word and human response to it. The church's purpose is teaching persons how to listen to the Word and how to respond—teaching persons to whom to pray, how to pray, and for what to pray. The church that fulfills this mission is a church that is faithful and vital.

An Invitation to Honesty

Intimacy entails being exposed. We are known for who and what we are. This is especially true for intimacy with God. Can we be anything other than honest with God? Because the One to whom we pray knows the number of hairs on our heads as well as the thoughts of our hearts, what do we hope to gain by maintaining our pretenses and facades?

Like most pastors, I have the habit of asking persons whom I visit in the hospital if they want me to pray with them. I assume that church members expect it of their pastor. Moreover, the bedside prayer is a convenient way to conclude the visit and make an exit. (Maybe my hospital visits would be as spiritual as they are social if we were to pray at the beginning of the visit rather than at the end.)

I recall one hospital visit in particular. We had chatted for a while and, after finding out he was likely to recover from his bout of pneumonia, I asked him if he wanted me to pray with him. He answered, no. No one had ever answered no before.

This man's honesty left me speechless. I was too startled by his departure from the expected polite response to explore his answer with him, so I awkwardly said good-bye and shuffled out the door. I carried his answer down the hospital corridor and much farther.

His answer remains with me to this day. Why did he refuse my offer to pray with him? Doesn't he believe in prayer? Doesn't he at least believe in pretending he believes in prayer? These questions about him have become questions about me, about us, and about our church. What do I, we, the church believe about prayer? His honesty, however disarming, invites our honesty. If we are honest, many of us will admit that we are not as convinced of the power of prayer as was James (James 5:13-18).

We can blame our cultural milieu for our ambivalence about prayer. Few escape its rationalism, scientific objectivity, and bottom-line pragmatism. We are encouraged to be skeptical about what is beyond our control. Reality and truth are confined within the borders of this world. Furthermore, we are concerned about productivity. Our aim is to get the job done. Subsequently, on the one hand prayer is perceived and employed as a kind of magical stardust to be sprinkled over life's unmanageable crises, and on the other hand it is rejected by the informed and the resourceful as an exercise engaged in by only the unsophisticated and weak.

Where We Usually Begin

What usually prompts our honest reflection on prayer are questions about its effectiveness. We would prefer to avoid the hard questions that prayer raises. Afraid of discrediting prayer for others as well as ourselves, we believers are tempted to sweep our doubts and questions under the proverbial rug. If we don't mention them in public, then maybe they will go away.

Listen carefully to some of our questions about prayer and see if you detect an ulterior motive.

What should we pray for?
Why are some of our prayers unanswered?
Why does it seem that we have changed God's mind
    when our prayers are answered, and how can that be?
Do we know more about our needs than God does?
When good things happen, how much credit is due to our
    human efforts, and how much is due to the God to
    whom we pray?

Did you hear the ulterior motive? Our questions about prayer usually are prompted by a concern about ourselves, our wants, our agenda.

One Ministers' Week at Emory University—the annual homecoming of the theology school's graduates—boasted a series of lectures by several "big names" from the church and academia. The theme was the Holy Spirit, and Oral Roberts was the biggest of the big names—especially for his followers, who packed the balcony of Glenn Memorial Church on the edge of the Emory campus.

An afternoon panel discussion including all the lecturers quickly became a dialogue between Roberts and Krister Stendahl, who was then dean of Harvard Divinity School. This question was posed: What are we to pray for? Are we to pray for parking spaces close to the door and for lost shoes?

Roberts was first to answer. He said, "I believe God loves us so much that he is concerned about everything we're concerned about, including our need for parking spaces and lost shoes." The balcony exploded with applause. When the dust settled, Stendahl replied, "Yes, but I think God would have us be concerned about things bigger than parking spaces and lost shoes."

Stendahl's reply shifted our reflection on prayer from ourselves to God. What would God have us be concerned about? We cannot answer this question without first considering the God to whom we pray.

We are destined to be theologians. That is, each of us possesses some understanding of who God is and of the nature of God's relationship with us. When we reach this understanding intentionally, we are aware not only of who God is but also of why we lay claim to this particular belief. Frequently, however, we abdicate our belief to others who, in effect, are permitted to do our thinking about God for us. Our choice, then, is whether we will carry on the theological task intentionally or abdicate it to others.

Several years ago J. B. Phillips wrote the popular book *Your God Is Too Small*. By depicting one common conceptualization after another, he sought to show that most of our ideas about God are too small. If our God is too small, then our prayer also is too small. For example, if our prayer is selfish, it is because we assume that we pray to a God who endorses our self-centeredness and self-indulgence. Or if our prayer is parochial, it is a reflection of our perception of a God whose sovereignty is limited to our loves and loyalties. As our understanding of God goes, so goes our understanding of prayer and praying.

A New Beginning

If we are to begin our understanding of prayer with who God is and what God has done rather than with ulterior motives regarding prayer's usefulness for our purposes, then we must learn a new language. Our confession will be that of Isaiah: "Woe is me! I am lost, for I am a man of unclean lips, and I live among a people of unclean lips" (Isaiah 6:5*a*). Our "normal" speech is permeated with sin and evil.

The only way to speak this new language is, as Jeremiah put it, to have the law of God written upon our hearts (Jeremiah 31:32). God's law is written upon our hearts when we hear God's voice. To hear God's voice and recognize it requires that we learn God's language; and we learn God's language the same way we learn all speech—by being spoken to. We learn God's language through the conversation God has with us. As a result of what God has said and is saying, we learn how to pray.

In Acts 2, the Holy Spirit came upon the believers who were gathered in Jerusalem on Pentecost. One of the strange experiences manifesting the Spirit's active presence was their ability to communicate across language barriers.

Now there were devout Jews from every nation under heaven living in Jerusalem. And at this sound the crowd gathered and was bewildered, because each one heard them speaking in the native language of each. Amazed and astonished, they asked, "Are not all these who are speaking Galileans? And how is it that we hear, each of us, in our own native language? . . . In our own languages we hear them speaking about God's deeds of power." All were amazed and perplexed, saying to one another, "What does this mean?" (Acts 2:5-8, 11-12)

What this means is that when we speak God's language, when we pray, we are doing what the church is called to do—to speak about God's deeds of power. When we pray, we not only speak about God's deeds of power, but we also become God's deeds of power. What follows is intended to help individuals and congregations become God's deeds of power.

Prayer: Our Conversation with God

L et us start with the basics. Prayer is speech. It consists of words. Paul observed, "We do not know how to pray as we ought, but that very Spirit intercedes with sighs too deep for words" (Romans 8:26*b*). Yet our sighs are preliminary to words, much as our tears are preliminary to words.

At an early age we learn how to talk by being spoken to. What we hear shapes what we think and say. It might be said that something doesn't exist until it has a name. Likewise, our experience doesn't make sense until it fits into a frame of reference or order that has been constructed of words. These words form a language that creates a world of meaning.

If I do not know your language, I cannot enter your world. For example, if you are computer literate and begin to speak of megabytes and modems, my response will be "It's Greek to me!" Because I have not learned computer language, the world of computers is foreign to me.

When we are spoken to, we not only receive a language that creates a world of meaning by which we make sense of life, but we also receive ourselves. We are shaped, in large part, by the words that are spoken to us and by the way they are spoken. Words are like hands on clay; they form their hearers.

When I was eight years old, I weighed over one hundred pounds. In other words, I was fat. The kids in the neighborhood nicknamed me Rumpy. In my memory the name is accompanied by an incident involving one of my friends and his mother. (At least I was *told* it involved his mother!) We'd built a treehouse. Upon its completion, I was informed by my friend that his mother did not want me in the treehouse whenever any of the other kids were in it. She was afraid it might collapse under my weight. The humiliation stuck with me. Since junior high, I've been a runner. I have no doubt that this is due, in part, to my desire to control my weight and to never be called Rumpy again.

For better or worse, speech is creative. It shapes us. It produces worlds of meaning wherein certain responses can be expected.

Regardless of what else we may want to say about prayer, prayer is speech. We speak to the One who first spoke to us. God's speech brought us into being. God's language provides us a world of meaning in which to understand ourselves and our world.

God Began the Conversation

In the beginning God spoke, and the heavens and the earth came into being. This was not just any earth that

God created; this was a particular world with a particular order. "Let there be light," God said, and there was light. Creation turned out the way it did because of the particular words God spoke to bring it into being. This phenomenon of creating from speech is not foreign to us; our marriages, families, churches, and even our nations become what they are as a result of the words spoken by and to those within them. Words have the power to create reality.

Humankind also was created in a particular way—in the image of God. We were given the capacity to speak and, with our speaking, to create and give order to what otherwise would be senseless experience.

After creating male and female, God said to them, "Be fruitful and multiply, and fill the earth and subdue it; and have dominion over the fish of the sea and over the birds of the air and over every living thing that moves upon the earth" (Genesis 1:28). And how was this to be achieved? In part, it was to be through speech: "So out of the ground the Lord God formed every animal of the field and every bird of the air, and brought them to the man to see what he would call them; and whatever the man called every living creature, that was its name" (Genesis 2:19). Men and women were created to be partners with God in Creation through the ordering power of speech.

John begins his Gospel with a reference to Creation: "In the beginning was the Word, and the Word was with God, and the Word was God" (1:1). The Greek word meaning "Word" is *logos*—from which we get the word *logic*. Thus, in the beginning was God's logic, by which life is to make sense or have meaning. In the beginning

God had a plan for Creation. This determined the way life was ordered.

God ordered the world so that those who were made a little lower than the angels would be in communion with God through words, through speech, through conversation. Prayer, then, is the way we are to relate to God. God speaks; we answer. Prayer is our listening and our answering.

Our Response

My friend Nancy called to tell me about her brother. He had been diagnosed as having throat cancer. The prognosis was bleak. She told me, "I knew he was losing weight. He had been growing weaker for some time. I could tell his voice was not what it once was. If I'd only been more attentive, I could have seen the symptoms and suggested earlier that he go to a doctor."

In Genesis and then in John's Gospel, God's order for life is revealed to be conversational. God speaks, and we are created. We are created in such a way that we may answer. But we must be attentive to the One who attends to us. If we are not attentive, we will miss what God is saying, and, in God's apparent absence from us, we will become absent from God.

Prayer is being as God is—attentive and eager to enjoy relationship. Prayer is our response to what God has said and is saying. Prayer is natural in the sense that it expresses our relationship with the One to whom we belong. It is the communication of child with parent and parent with child. This communication produces communion, which is oneness between those who would otherwise be separate.

When we are attentive, our life becomes a response to God. Our life becomes prayer. We pray "without ceasing" when we are aware of this sacred relationship in which all our being and doing abides; and when we pray without ceasing, we give witness to our desire for the holy communion that existed "in the beginning."

Imagine how it was between God and humankind in the Garden of Eden. I imagine it was like those precious and rare moments when the barriers of our material and sinful existence are penetrated by an experience of oneness, of communion with God and people. Misunderstanding gives way to understanding. Heart speaks to heart. We might call it "being on the same wavelength."

In the Garden, what God had in mind for men and women governed the way men and women lived. God's thoughts were their thoughts. God's ways were their ways. They enjoyed a holy communion.

They enjoyed a holy communion until an "ordering word" other than God's Word was spoken and heard. An alien voice taught God's own children a foreign language. With this foreign language came a different world than the one God intended. A new order for governing life was introduced. "You will be like God," the serpent said seductively. It got humankind's attention!

The Conversation Was Interrupted

God spoke and called creation into being. God spoke and made us to live in communion with God and with one another. Our humanity and our holiness depend on our hearing and responding to God's Word. Our life thrives on our conversation with God.

But the conversation was interrupted. Humankind's attention was distracted. The serpent asked the woman, "Did God say, 'You shall not eat from any tree in the garden'?" The woman said to the serpent, "We may eat of the fruit of the trees in the garden, but God said, 'You shall not eat of the fruit of the tree that is in the middle of the garden, nor shall you touch it, or you shall die'" (Genesis 3:1b-3).

God's words are remembered. Our memory permits the God-human conversation to continue from the past to the present. What God once said echoes in our ears as though it were being said to us for the first time.

The serpent attempted to undermine the communion God and humankind enjoyed. God's Word was questioned. That is, God's order for governing humankind's behavior was challenged by another order. "The serpent said to the woman, 'You will not die; for God knows that when you eat the fruit of the tree, your eyes will be opened, and you will be like God, knowing good and evil' " (Genesis 3:4).

The man and woman listened to this voice that was not God's voice. They would have access to the knowledge of good and evil and, thus, would not have to depend upon God to reveal it to them. It was as if the serpent said, "Listen to me and you will be able to listen to yourselves. You will no longer need God to give you your identity and your world of meaning. You will be able to do that for yourselves."

Humankind's conversation with this foreign voice caused a new language to be learned and a new world to be created. The original world became a world characterized by fear, shame, deception, and blame—a world where communion had become disunion.

But God did not end the conversation, despite humankind's disloyalty. "The Lord God called to the man, and said to him, 'Where are you?' He said, 'I heard the sound of you in the garden, and I was afraid, because I was naked; and I hid myself.' He said, 'Who told you that you were naked? Have you eaten from the tree of which I commanded you not to eat?' " (Genesis 3:9-11). The man blamed the woman. More precisely, he blamed God for giving him the woman. Then the woman blamed the serpent. "He tricked me," she said.

Life would never be the same again. Paradise was lost. Intimacy was shattered. What once was whole now was broken. Communication once pure and true now was perverted. Words now were used to tempt, manipulate, deceive, cover up, and blame. The consequence was shame and fear, which merely perpetuated the vicious cycle of temptation, manipulation, deception, and blaming.

Our Corrupt Language and World

The language of God's original world engenders trust; the language of the serpent's world engenders distrust and fear. The language of God's original world produces clarity and transparency; the language of the serpent's world produces distortion and deception. The language of God's original world nurtures intimacy; the language of the serpent's world causes estrangement.

Listen. Whose language do you hear being spoken?

Whose language do you speak? Is it the language learned from God or from the Evil One?

I don't know about you, but I tend to become depressed during political campaigns. What such local and national exercises in democracy do for me is portray vividly how estranged we are from one another and how exploitative of others we will be to get what we want.

We do not know the candidates, so they hire media consultants who use words and visual images that pollsters have determined will be perceived favorably by the electorate. Politicians learn which words can be pushed as buttons to obtain allegiance and win the election. For example, despite the fact that a politician's own family life may be in shambles, he or she may make "the family" central to campaign rhetoric because it will play well with the voters. In the serpent's world, words are used to deceive and manipulate.

Words can be used to build up or to tear down. The problem in the serpent's world is that we're never sure how the words are being used. Too often words are used to hurt, cripple, and destroy. We use words to hurt others. Others use words to hurt us. Sometimes we even use words to hurt ourselves. Unaware, we use words to imprison ourselves.

I know a woman. Maybe you know her, too. She talks so incessantly that you can't get a word in edgewise. It is as if she is afraid to listen. I think she is afraid of hearing a truth that she is not able to handle or control. That truth might tell her that she can be more than she has been, which she probably suspects. It might tell her that her efforts to control people and situations are unnecessary. It might invite her to trust God and those whom she believes she must fear. It might help her to see that the foxhole she digs with her nonstop talking is really a prison. Instead of protecting her, her talking is preventing her from receiving what she so desperately needs: God's Word and its intimacy.

What may be most tragic is that even our religious language, even our prayer, is not immune to the influence of the Evil One. Instead of being language that creates and reconciles, prayer often becomes another means to the serpent's ends of self-aggrandizement, competition, separation, and isolation.

Jesus' instruction regarding prayer in the Sermon on the Mount addresses the hypocrites who "love to stand and pray in the synagogues and at the street corners, so that they may be seen by others" (Matthew 6:5b). He also addresses the Gentiles who "heap up empty phrases . . . for they think that they will be heard because of their many words" (6:7).

This kind of prayer is corrupt because it is used to impress others with one's piety and religiosity. If verbosity works in the world, then why not try it on God? Jesus says no. When it comes to speech, whether it be in the courts or in prayer, "Let your word be 'Yes, Yes' or 'No, No'; anything more than this comes from the evil one" (Matthew 5:37). Say what you mean and mean what you say. Be honest. Be true.

Likewise, the prayer of the Pharisee in Luke 18:9-14 is unacceptable because the Pharisee's words assume that his relationship with the tax collector is a comparison based on inherent judgmentalism: "God, I thank you that I am not like other people: thieves, rogues, adulterers, or even like this tax collector" (verse 11b).

The Pharisee's words put distance between himself and the tax collector.

God's Word, on the other hand, seeks to close the distance, to replace estrangement with reconciliation. Jesus says to Matthew, "Come, follow me. Be one of my own." To Zacchaeus Jesus says, "I want to fellowship with you in your house tonight."

Not only can our prayer become corrupt, but even our spiritual language can become corrupt. In 1 Corinthians 12–14, Paul addresses those Christians who are using *glossolalia,* speaking in tongues, as a yardstick for measuring spiritual superiority within the Christian community. Paul asserts, "If I speak in the tongues of mortals and of angels, but do not have love, I am a noisy gong or a clanging cymbal" (13:1).

Our prayer and spiritual language can be influenced by the Evil One just as all speech can. I've used such language, and you probably have, too.

I'll pray for you.
Translation: Will you please leave so I can get on to more important things?

May I pray with you? (spoken by the pastor beside the hospital bed)
Translation: I've got three other people to see, so I need to bring this visit to a close.

I've prayed about this.
Translation: I've argued my point. You've argued yours. Since I've prayed about it, I must be right. How dare you disagree with me!

Let's pray about this.
Translation: It's obvious a response is called for, but the risk is too great. Prayer will be safer than action.

If even our spiritual language and prayer are prone to being corrupt, is there any hope for us? Is there a Word from God?

Yes, there is! In fact, the Word of God was made flesh and came to live with us.

The Conversation Is Restored

Saint Augustine's prayer depicts our human condition when we are apart from God: "You awaken us to delight in your praises; for you made us for yourself, and our heart is restless until it reposes in you" (Horton Davies, ed., *The Communion of Saints: Prayers of the Famous* [Grand Rapids: Eerdmans, 1990], p. 17). We yearn for intimacy with the One who created us—the One to whom we belong and in whom we live and move and have our being. Without God, we are lost. Something crucial is missing. We are not right. Our hearts are restless.

We yearn for a word from God, but the language and world of the Evil One doom us to a constricted conversation. We are limited to talking to ourselves, and the vocabulary we use consists of words such as *self-sufficiency, self-preservation, self-justification,* and *self-defense.*

Yet despite our emphasis on the self, the self remains discontent. All our efforts are self-defeating. What starts

with the self ends with the self and with others—as
limited as when it began. The self discovers it cannot
ascertain what it needs most. The self discovers it is not
God after all. The self cannot save itself; its hope lies
beyond itself.

The good news is that the One we need comes seeking
us. As John put it, "For God so loved the world that he
gave his only Son, so that everyone who believes in him
may not perish but may have eternal life" (John 3:16).
Into the babble of humanity's confused and perverse
speech, God's own Word is presented in the flesh.

The Word was present "in the beginning":

> In the beginning was the Word, and the Word was with
> God, and the Word was God. He was in the beginning
> with God. All things came into being through him, and
> without him not one thing came into being. . . . And the
> Word became flesh and lived among us, and we have
> seen his glory, the glory as of a father's only son, full of
> grace and truth. (John 1:1-3, 14)

Into the world's darkness Jesus, God's incarnate
Word, shines. His illumination exposes the world's
foreign language to be that of the Evil One. He teaches
the world the language of God's world, the language of
the kingdom of heaven.

Jesus is the messenger—and the message. His words
speak as loudly as his actions, for he reveals to the world
what it is to be true and whole—a person of integrity. He
enjoys communion with God. There is no hypocrisy, no
lie, in him.

A New Language for a New World

Jesus is full of grace and truth. His words and his actions teach the world the language of the kingdom of heaven. The vocabulary of this language consists of words such as *self-denial, self-giving,* and *self-sacrifice*—opposites of those the Evil One speaks and teaches.

The serpent promised Adam and Eve that they would be like God by eating of the tree of knowledge. But Jesus revealed that we are like God when we become vulnerable in the name of love. Being right—the consequence of knowing good and evil—does not make us like God. Being loving does.

Loving requires self-denial, self-giving, and self-sacrifice. It requires identification with those who are loved. Love is Emmanuel, God with us. Paul explains what is required by this kind of love when he describes Jesus as one "who, though he was in the form of God, did not regard equality with God as something to be exploited, but emptied himself, taking the form of a slave, being born in human likeness. And being found in human form, he humbled himself and became obedient to the point of death—even death on a cross" (Philippians 2:6-8).

Jesus revealed *to* the world how much it is loved. Jesus also revealed *for* the world how communion is restored. Communion comes through "emptying"— through sympathy with others, through humble service, and through obedience, even unto death.

Two key images of the new language are the cross and the empty tomb. By giving one's life away in obedience to God's love, one's life is restored. The world which lives by the old language of self-preservation finds this new language incomprehensible. It doesn't make sense. It sounds illogical—and, of course, it is, unless one understands life by God's *logos,* God's Word, God's logic, which is revealed to the world through Jesus.

In the world of the kingdom of heaven, the last are first and the first are last. The poor have good news preached to them, and the rich are sent away empty. "Love your enemies and pray for those who persecute you," Jesus says.

In the world of the kingdom of heaven, death is no longer feared. The Evil One enforces his rule by the threat of death, but God's Word reveals that the final word is life, not death. It is Easter, not Good Friday.

By faith in Christ we die to sin and the power of death, and we are raised to a new life. We are born again—this time from above. Freed from death's chains, we are no longer anxious about life's perceived and real necessities. We are no longer slaves to expediency for the sake of our personal welfare. We trust the One who made us and to whom we belong. The God who feeds the sparrows and clothes the lilies of the field provides for us.

Freed from ourselves, we are able to find ourselves by losing ourselves in love. We are free to love because we have been loved. God's Word made flesh told us and showed us. Through Jesus the conversation is restored. Through Jesus our restless hearts find their repose in God. We live according to the order God intended.

The Power of Prayer

Paul's confession is my own: "When I was a child, I spoke like a child, I thought like a child, I reasoned like a child; when I became an adult, I put an end to childish ways" (1 Corinthians 13:11). As a boy, I often prayed for the opposite of what I wanted. Because it seemed that I never got what I wanted, I decided to pray for what I didn't want in order to receive what I did want. When the parental no comes too frequently, why not ask for the opposite of what is really desired so that the anticipated no, in actuality, will be yes?

The alternative to such games is to stop asking altogether. Prayer, like all speech, is offered with the expectation that it will be heard and responded to. Something in us dies when we stop trying to be heard and responded to. Perhaps it is the image of God.

But prayer is not our manipulation of God to get what we want. The quantity of our prayers will not ensure that we get what we ask for. Fasting will not guarantee the efficacy of our prayers either. Manipulation is not a part of Jesus' vocabulary. To call him Lord and to pray in his name is to be committed to his rule for life. The rule by which he taught, lived, and died is not manipulative, coercive, deceitful, or coy. Our prayer, therefore, cannot be these things.

When we pray for God's kingdom to come and God's will to be done on earth as it is in heaven, we cannot pray for what is contrary to God's kingdom and will. The power of prayer—that is, what prayer does—must be understood in the context of God's kingdom and will.

God's *logos*, the "law and order" of the kingdom of heaven, is revealed through word and deed by Jesus. Today it is actualized through the power of the Holy Spirit. Therefore, the power of prayer is equal to the power of the Holy Spirit. What we can expect prayer to do is what we believe the Holy Spirit does: empower those who are being saved from the power of the Evil One to live the Truth of Jesus.

The Power of the Holy Spirit

In Jesus we see as well as hear God's Word, which sets us free. His Spirit, the very life of God, is given to us so that ours is not a theoretical liberation but a real one. In the cross we see the Evil One's way for what it really is, and we are not damned to inevitably live it. In the cross we also see the love of One whose identification with us is so complete that he suffers and dies on account of our sin. As a result, our hearts are changed. We want to love as we've been loved. We want the logic of the amazing grace that "saves a wretch like me" to govern our feeling, willing, and living.

We can better understand the power of the Spirit—and thus the power of our prayer—by considering the biblical witness to what the Spirit does.

The Holy Spirit sends believers to address sin by calling persons to repent of their sin and by assuring persons that God has forgiven them. According to John's Gospel, Jesus gave the Holy Spirit to the disciples on Easter evening as they gathered together behind locked doors. Jesus appeared to them and said, " 'Peace be with you. As the Father has sent me, so I send you.' When he had said this, he breathed on them and said to them, 'Receive the Holy Spirit. If you forgive the sins of any, they are forgiven them; if you retain the sins of any, they are retained' " (20:21-23).

The Holy Spirit breaks down the barriers that inhibit communicating the Good News of God in Christ. In Luke's account, the Holy Spirit descends upon the believers in Jerusalem on Pentecost. The Spirit is given not as a gentle breath, but as a mighty wind, fire, and extraordinary speech. People from all over the known world hear their native languages as the Galileans speak.

Through Jesus a new language is revealed to the world. Through the Holy Spirit, believers are given the power to speak it. It is the language of love. Love will find a way through the barriers that divide and separate.

The Holy Spirit provides the courage and the words to witness to the mighty deeds of God—even in threatening situations. Jesus promised it: "When they bring you before the synagogues, the rulers, and the authorities, do not worry about how you are to defend yourselves or what you are to say; for the Holy Spirit will teach you at that very hour what you ought to say" (Luke 12:11-12).

The Holy Spirit reminds us of what we have forgotten as well as teaches us truths we have not learned. Jesus promised to send a Helper who "will teach you everything, and remind you of all that I have said to you" (John 14:26*b*). The Spirit reminds us of our baptism, when we first heard God's Word spoken to us and God's Truth spoken about us. The Spirit reminds us that we do not belong to the Evil One, even when we begin to think and act as if we do.

The Holy Spirit gives gifts to members of the Body of Christ in order to edify the church and enable its mission and ministry in the world. In three of his letters, Paul refers to these gifts in terms of both capabilities and roles (Romans 12; 1 Corinthians 12; Ephesians 3). The capabilities include healing, assistance, leadership, speaking in tongues, prophesying, ministering, giving generously, and showing compassion. Among the roles he names are apostles, prophets, teachers, evangelists, and pastors.

Other works, or powers, of the Holy Spirit could be cited. Permit the preceding five examples to show how God's power is active in the world. To pray in Jesus' name is to pray for the Spirit to continue its saving and sanctifying ministry. To speak of the power of prayer is to refer to what happens when we want what God wants and submit ourselves to God for its actualization.

What Shall We Pray For?

Recognizing the power of prayer through the power of the Holy Spirit, what, then, shall we pray for? Shall we pray for parking spaces and lost shoes? Surely God loves us enough to care about our smallest needs. The issue, however, is not whether God cares about what we care about but whether we care about what God cares about.

If the things we pray for are not means to the end of our service to God, do they not have the ring of "When I was a child, I spoke like a child"? The story of what God has done in Jesus and the Holy Spirit reveals God to be about something of cosmic proportions. Don't parking spaces, lost shoes, winning athletic contests, doing well on the exam, and being chosen beauty pageant queen all pale in the shadow of the cross? Don't they sound like the serpent's language of self-interest and self-preoccupation?

I am frequently asked to pray at football games. I must admit that I agonize over what to say. What does one pray for at the beginning of a football game? After quickly discarding the notion of praying for victory, I'm tempted to pray that the athletes will be kept safe from physical harm. Although I certainly want no one to get hurt, as I listen to the God to whom I pray, I hear God answer, "If you're so concerned about no one getting hurt, then why not suggest they play touch instead of tackle?" What sense does it make to pray that God will spare us the consequences of our needless and frivolous risks?

If our prayer is no longer "Give me, give me" (because Jesus tells us to give to others), then what should it be? If our prayer is no longer "Defeat my enemies" (because Jesus tells us to love them), then what are we to pray for? If our prayer is no longer "Spare me, while others suffer" (because Jesus shows us that suffering can be redemptive), then what is our prayer to be?

It comes as no surprise that the disciples also wondered what those who live in the new world of the kingdom of heaven are supposed to want and what language will best express their love for the One who loves them and offers them a new way of living. So the disciples said to Jesus, "Lord, teach us to pray" (Luke 11:1-4; Matthew 6:9-13).

Jesus taught the disciples, and us, to pray. This prayer helps us to see what those who are in conversation, in communion, with God want and live for. Those who have heard God's Word and who believe in him live in this world with their eyes and hearts on God's world. They not only want what God wants, but they also actualize what God wants through the power of the Holy Spirit. God's will *will* be done on earth as it is in heaven by the power of prayer, which comes by the power of the Holy Spirit. But what is God's will? What does God want?

God wants communion with humankind. Jesus says, "When you pray, say, 'Our Father in heaven. . . . ' " The relationship wherein we pray is like that of parent and child. A parent teaches a child to speak by speaking to her. God teaches us to speak by speaking to us. What we hear is God's Word, Jesus Christ. Jesus reveals the trustworthiness of God.

Because God is "our" Father, the relationship entails our solidarity, our communion, with all the Father's children. To add "in heaven" is to acknowledge that those relationships are primary. The One to whom we pray, who makes us one with humankind, has no equal on earth.

God wants the original order of creation to be

restored. To say "Hallowed be your name" is to acknowledge that God is God—and we are not. God is sovereign over all Creation. To hallow God's name is to do the opposite of taking God's name in vain. To want God's name to be hallowed is to want all creation to join the chorus praising God for being God—and thus assume its relative position to the Creator.

God wants to replace the present governance of the world with the rule of love. To say "Your kingdom come. Your will be done, on earth as it is in heaven" is to acknowledge that the earth suffers from corruption. This is no easy confession, for we may be benefiting so much from the present order that its flaws are imperceptible to us. Why should we want God's kingdom to come when the present one serves us quite adequately?

God wants our trust in order to give us heaven's peace. To say "Give us this day our daily bread" is to acknowledge that we are not self-sufficient. Yet we are not anxious. We trust God to provide for our needs. Because we pray in solidarity with all God's children, it is *our* need and not just one's own need or the need of one's group or one's nation.

God wants us to be free to love. To be free to love, we must not be weighted with our guilt, our obligations, or our debts. God wants to forgive us and wants us to forgive one another. To say "And forgive us our debts as we also have forgiven our debtors" is to confess that just as we need daily bread to sustain the body, so also we need daily grace to sustain the soul.

We are unable to right all the wrongs we've committed. We cannot fix everything we've broken. We cannot reverse all the harm we've done. We cannot compensate God for our conscious infidelities, much less for our unconscious ones. Our only hope is to be forgiven—to be treated in a way other than the way we deserve.

This petition recognizes that we are debtors together. We owe God and one another more than we can ever repay. Therefore, we all need to be forgiven. I cannot want forgiveness for myself alone. Since it is "our" Father to whom we pray, I cannot ask for myself alone what I know you also need. And because I need forgiveness from you, or from someone like you, how can I refuse you forgiveness? How can I expect from you what I am not willing to give you? As long as we withhold forgiveness from one another, disunity continues to undermine our community, and the body of which we are individual members is crippled. The rule of God cannot be realized fully until we seek forgiveness and forgive others.

God wants us to resist the Evil One. To say "And do not bring us to the time of trial, but rescue us from the evil one" is to acknowledge that we are Adam and Eve's descendants. Their distrust and disobedience is in our bloodstream. Like them, we still want to be like God.

When Jesus was tempted by the Devil in the wilderness, he resisted the Evil One's seduction by returning to the Word of God: "It is written, 'One does not live by bread alone, but by every word that comes from the mouth of God'" (Matthew 4:4). Our track record is one of succumbing to temptation. The Evil One's words cause us to forget God's Word. We are as easily tricked as Eve was.

We cannot break the hold that the Evil One has on us

by pulling ourselves up by our own spiritual bootstraps. To be sure, our will is involved, but we are not up to the test. We need more. Jesus teaches us to pray for what we need.

The prayer, as we are used to saying it, concludes the way it begins—with adoration and praise. To say "For yours is the kingdom and the power and the glory, forever and ever. Amen" is to break into a proclamation of faith and hope. God is *our* God. Our lives rest in this faith in the present time, and we believe it will be true for all time. God's world is without end. Amen.

How Shall We Pray?

We pray expecting a response. "Is there anyone among you who, if your child asks for bread, will give a stone? Or if the child asks for a fish, will give a snake? If you then, who are evil, know how to give good gifts to your children, how much more will your Father in heaven give good things to them who ask him!" (Matthew 7:9-11). We pray expecting the God who created us and loves us to respond to us. When we pray for God's will, God's saving grace, to work through us and throughout the whole earth, we pray with trust and confidence. Our faith is that God will respond because we care about what God already cares about.

Therefore, we do not pray with our fingers crossed. We do not hedge our prayers with loopholes and safeguards. When we pray that God's will be done, we trust that God will respond. Because God is God, and we are not, we cannot predict how God will respond. We just know, as well as we know anything, that God will respond.

The question is not whether God wants children with cancer to be cured, or starving nations to be fed, or violence to cease, or alcoholics to remain sober. Do we pray for the starving to be fed if we believe that it might be God's will for them to starve to death? No, we pray expecting a response, even a miracle. It is no less a miracle for the rich to share their wealth, the overfed their abundance, or the powerful their power to ensure that available food supplies are properly distributed than it is for manna to come from heaven. In fact, these things might be more of a miracle than manna from heaven.

A child dies of cancer. Populations starve to death. Relatives beat and kill one another. Nations invade other nations. An alcoholic falls off the wagon. Do we stop praying because it seems futile? Do we stop praying because the Evil One seems to have the upper hand?

Luke 18:1-8 is a story Jesus told about a widow who will not acquiese to a callous judge's refusal to grant her the justice she is due. At last he relents to rid himself of the nuisance. Jesus asks, "And will not God grant justice to his chosen ones who cry to him day and night? Will he delay long in helping them? I tell you, he will quickly grant justice to them. And yet, when the Son of Man comes, will he find faith on earth?" (verses 7-8).

Jesus' point is not that we can expect to badger God into fulfilling our requests. Rather, our God is just and will deliver justice. Our persistent prayer is evidence of our trust in God's promise never to forsake his children to the Evil One.

We may wonder, "Will he delay long in helping?" Sometimes it seems that way to us, but our sense of time is distorted by our vantage point in the present. Just as Jesus' experience of God-forsakenness on the cross must have seemed like an eternity, so our experiences of God's apparent absence in pain, injustice, loss, and failure seem like an eternity. Actually, Jesus' experience was temporary, and it shows us that ours is, too.

The question Jesus asks us is this: "When the Son of Man comes, will he find faith on earth?" Prayer is the means by which faith, hope, and love are kept alive. Remember that we are responding only to what we have heard and seen. The vocabulary of faith did not originate with us. We learned it through God's Word. Jesus taught it to us.

Are We to Pray for Healing?

Jesus healed the physically, psychologically, and spiritually sick. He healed the paralytic, the man born blind, the woman with the hemorrhage, Jairus's daughter, the Canaanite woman's daughter, the man possessed by demons, Simon's mother-in-law, the ten lepers, and others. When John sent his disciples to Jesus to ask if he was the Messiah, Jesus answered: "Go and tell John what you hear and see: the blind receive their sight, the lame walk, the lepers are cleansed, the deaf hear, the dead are raised, and the poor have good news brought to them. And blessed is anyone who takes no offense at me" (Matthew 11:4-6). By releasing persons from their pain, torment, and physical limitations and making them whole, Jesus demonstrated how things will be in the kingdom of heaven, which he prayed will come on earth.

Being freed from the power of the Evil One includes being released from self-preoccupation and separation from the community. Pain and infirmity make us self-preoccupied. Illness and disease separate us from the community.

Lest we suspect that the ministry of healing was limited to Jesus, recall the post-Pentecost experience of Peter and John at the temple. A man who had been lame from birth begged for alms. Peter replied, "I have no silver or gold, but what I have I give you; in the name of Jesus Christ of Nazareth, stand up and walk" (Acts 3:6). And he did. The apostles carried on the ministry of Jesus, and that ministry included healing.

Does our ministry today include healing, too? I believe it does. We pray and work for God's will to be done on earth as it is in heaven. This is as true for healing as for justice, hunger, and all our prayers for God's children. Our prayer reflects our faith in the Lord's promise. There is a day coming, says the Lord, when health will replace disease, when wholeness will replace brokenness, when the blind will see, when the deaf will hear, when the crippled will walk, when the mentally disturbed will receive peace. All things are possible with God. Healing cannot be excluded.

What About Unanswered Prayer?

We are persistent in our praying. We believe we are asking for God's will, not just our own. Why, then, do our prayers go unanswered?

Recall Paul's prayer asking God to remove his "thorn in the flesh" (2 Corinthians 12:7). We don't know what

Paul's thorn in the flesh was. Because he referred to it as a "messenger from Satan," some have supposed it to be some kind of psychological or spiritual affliction. Maybe it was a specific temptation or sin he was susceptible to. Others have supposed it to be something physical: a speech defect, a stomach disorder, weak eyesight, epilepsy, tuberculosis, unattractive appearance.

Whatever his thorn in the flesh was, it was, for him, a source of humility, if not humiliation. Although he eventually was able to talk about it positively, we can read between the lines of his second letter to the Corinthians and tell that, along the way, Paul viewed it as a hindrance to his ministry. Paul confessed to having prayed three times to the Lord that his torment might leave him. God responded, "My grace is sufficient for you, for my power is made perfect in weakness" (12:9).

Now what kind of answer is that? It is a strange answer, especially to those who believe that God is supposed to answer our prayers if we ask for something good. Surely Paul's healing qualified as something good. So why didn't Paul get what he prayed for?

Some respond to the problem of unanswered prayer by saying that it is merely a matter of our limited perspective. Our present is but a blip on the timeline of eternity. Thus, when we say that our prayer is unanswered, what we are really saying is that it is unanswered thus far. It hasn't been answered *yet*. From this point of view, there is no such thing as unanswered prayers—just impatient pray-ers.

Another way to address the problem of unanswered prayer is to argue that God answers all our prayers; that is, God responds to our cries for help in ways we are not expecting. God responds, but it is not the response we would like to be given.

Some might say God answered Paul, and the answer was no. But the answer was more than no. God's response was "My grace is sufficient for you, for my power is made perfect in weakness" (12:9).

Despite all the miracles attributed to the power of the Holy Spirit, the key to understanding how that power is used lies in what it is used for. It is used to give witness to a life freed from the Evil One. Miracles are a means to the end of converting people to the reign of God's love.

What we tend to forget, perhaps because it is so painful for us to remember, is that God's love is most vividly displayed in Christ on the cross. God's love is revealed in submission, obedience, weakness, rejection, suffering, ridicule, and death. God's salvation comes not through military might or political power; it comes through sacrificial love. God's power is made perfect in weakness. It is a weakness that one assumes when one identifies with those who are powerless.

Paul prayed for healing. What he received was an invitation to trust God's grace all the more. His trust in God would turn his weakness from a liability to an asset. Exactly how this would happen Paul probably could not envision—at first. But after proceeding by faith, he was able to look back and see what God had done and was doing.

Because we listen as well as speak when we pray, we receive answers that may not seem like answers because they are not the answers we want. Sometimes the answer is healing. Pain and limitation are removed, and health and wholeness are restored. Sometimes, however, the answer comes through grace sufficient to make our witness to God in and through the pain and limitation that remain—and sometimes grow worse.

Because God's will is for the world to know liberation from the Evil One and life in the kingdom of heaven, it is our witness to such liberation that is most important. In some cases, the most effective witness is the miracle of physical healing. In other cases, the most effective witness is the miracle of victorious perseverance in the face of pain and limitation. What must remain unanswered is why God's grace takes one form for one person and another form for another.

Gloria and Bob are members of a church I once served. Gloria is confined to a wheelchair because she suffers from rheumatoid arthritis. Bob must dress her, help her get in and out of her wheelchair, and cut up her food for her. Bob is handsome, robust, and active. I once asked him if he resented Gloria's dependence on him. He replied, "How can I have a negative attitude about it when Gloria doesn't? Her cheerfulness and courage are an inspiration to me."

God is using Gloria as a means of grace even though her healing must wait until the life to come. Until then, both she and Bob are witnesses to how it is to be freed from the Evil One and to live by the logic of God.

A Personal Experience of Answered Prayer

Each of us is "put together" in a different way. Each of us is a case in point of the unresolved debate regarding the influences of heredity and environment. On the one hand are the influences of heredity: our size, appear-

ance, IQ, and athletic or artistic ability. On the other
hand are the influences of environment: the significant
others in our lives, the institutions in whose care we are
placed, the decisions that we make and that others make
for us, the "breaks" defined as opportunities that fall into
our laps inexplicably, and the "breaks" defined as
accidents, tragedies, and crises which hurt and scar. The
givens of our lives are stirred up in ways that sometimes
seem providential and other times seem haphazard. The
chemistry produces our predisposition—the way our
feeling, thinking, being, and doing are bent.

I was bent to be a perfectionist, to excel, to be
obsessed with what others thought of me. This particular
bent made me extremely responsible, which made me a
controlling person. As long as I maintained control, I
could be sure that things were done right. This would
ensure that people would think well of me. Afraid of
failure and its subsequent criticism, I felt compelled to
be all things to all people. To disappoint them would be
to risk their rejection and withdrawal of love. I would go
from being a somebody to being a nobody.

This drivenness—which included perfectionism in
appearance, morality, and performance—reached the
point where it was killing me. I could never do enough.
To meet one set of expectations only led to another set.
There was always that one person whom I had
displeased or to whom I had not proven my worth. I
could never rest. I could never do enough. As much as I
tried to control my life, I actually had little control. I was
driven, and I wasn't the driver.

This drivenness made me chronically fatigued. My
energy—my life—was consumed in either laboring to do

good or worrying that I had failed. I was susceptible to depression. At times I felt that if my life was destined to be lived this way, I wanted it to end.

I had named my sin, my brokenness, long ago. Acknowledging the powers that have us in their grasp is a crucial first step, but more is required for us to be set free. Accepting who we are can lead to despair if we believe we are powerless against the powers that bind us.

I remember the occasion well. I was involved with other Christians in a two-year experience called the Academy of Spiritual Formation. A healing service was held as part of Holy Communion. We were invited to meet with two persons whom we could ask to pray for us. If we desired, they would anoint us with oil, making the sign of the cross on our foreheads. Although I believe our prayers are not always answered the way we want them to be, I was open to receiving an answer to my prayer for healing.

It occurred to me that God wanted my release from bondage to my excessive drive and self-doubt as much as I did. It was one of those thoughts that, in retrospect, can best be described as grace-inspired. That God loved me, even me, and wanted my healing was good news to my heart as well as my mind. I dared to confess my need to the two who knelt beside me and prayed with me and for me.

I cannot explain what happened, but then the matters of prayer cannot be fully explained; they are to be received gratefully and witnessed to. So I witness to the mystery and the reality of prayer's power.

Since that healing service, my life has been different—at least it feels different to me. Yes, I still relapse into my former ways and become obsessive and compulsive about my performance and how others are judging it. Yes, I'm still considered by my family to be a workaholic who is preoccupied much of the time. I still give my children reason to say, "Earth to Daddy, Earth to Daddy," in order to remind me that wherever I may be, I'm not "with" them. But I am much more self-accepting, because I believe that deep within my being God accepts me and loves me unconditionally. I do not have to be perfect—just faithful. I do not have to be all things to all people. The truth is, it is usually better for them if I don't try to be.

I've tried the Evil One's alternative—trying to be like God—and it almost killed me. Now I'd rather receive God's gift than take God's place. It is an answer to prayer—an answer that is witness to the power of prayer.

The Purposes of Prayer

Despite all I have said about understanding prayer and its power, I must confess that prayer is a mystery. If what happens when you and I try to communicate with others defies control and comprehension, then surely prayer does as well.

Our attempts to understand prayer are similar to our attempts to understand the doctrine of the Trinity. We Protestants tend to see the doctrine as an analogy for the sake of gaining rational clarity. God is like a clover leaf, or a triangle, or a woman who is at the same time wife, mother, and doctor.

In the Eastern Orthodox tradition, the Trinity is not viewed as a conceptual device for wrapping our minds around God. Rather, it is just the opposite. The doctrine of the Trinity resists our attempts to gain control of God through our understanding. The doctrine's function is to keep us humble.

Just as the doctrine of the Trinity reminds us that God transcends our best explanations, so also the church's traditional understandings of prayer underscore prayer's mystery. The church experiences its conversation with God as having different purposes. Thus, prayer is described as adoration and praise, confession, intercession, petition, and thanksgiving. Each of these kinds of prayer is prophetic in the sense that it "goes against the grain" of our contemporary culture and its dominant ways of thinking, feeling, and acting.

Prayer Is Adoration and Praise

Adoration has a foreign ring to our ears. We call babies and puppies adorable, but that's about as close as we come to using the word today. Have we lost our capacity for adoration?

Adoration is our response to what is deserving of adoration. It is a natural response in that it cannot be forced. We adore God because we have experienced God as God. Adoration requires a personal encounter.

It was adoration that kept the Hebrews from speaking God's name when they read the Scriptures. When they came to *Yahweh* or *Jehovah*, they substituted *Adonai*, meaning *my Lord*. Moses took off his shoes when he approached the burning bush. In the temple Isaiah heard the heavenly chorus sing hymns of adoration: "Holy, holy, holy is the Lord of hosts; the whole earth is full of his glory" (Isaiah 6:3). On the mountain, Peter, James, and John saw the transfigured Jesus with Elijah and Moses. They heard God's voice from the cloud and fell to the ground. Adoration is spawned by awe.

In Mark's account of the Transfiguration, Peter interrupted the experience: "Rabbi, it is good for us to be here; let us make three dwellings, one for you, one for Moses, and one for Elijah" (9:5). Then Mark adds, "He did not know what to say, for they were terrified" (verse 6). Whatever is worthy of our adoration is full of terror. An appropriate response is reverent silence, but beneath the silence is the need to say something, however inadequate it may be. Peter spoke of building booths.

Peter's problem was how to respond to this awesome experience. Our problem is either that such experiences are no longer available to us or that we no longer permit ourselves to be available to such experiences. I believe it is the latter.

In *The Sacred Canopy*, Peter Berger observed that Protestants, in particular, have contributed to the increasing secularization of our culture. Reducing the sacraments to ordinances and removing the miracle of the mass, among other things, created what Berger termed the "disenchantment of the world." Mystery and miracle were lost. The umbilical cord between heaven and earth was cut. The only connection left was narrowly confined to God's written Word, the Bible. This set the stage for biblical literalism and fundamentalism.

According to biblical literalism, the words of the Bible are to be treated as if God were subsumed in them. One's relationship is with a book instead of with God. But what does prayer become when one no longer listens to the God who speaks through clouds, burning bushes, prophets and poets, and the still small voice as well as the biblical witnesses? If God already has said everything by way of the only link that now exists between heaven and earth—the Bible—then prayer is no longer a conversation; it is a human monologue.

Praise may be the way adoration best expresses itself when it opens its mouth and breaks the awe-inspired silence of a divine-human encounter, which may be precipitated by the biblical witnesses but cannot be reduced to them. But praise is as awkward for us to express as adoration is for us to experience.

When I recall instances when I have praised people because of who they are and not because of what they have done, I think of my children. I am sure they hear from me more words of criticism than words of praise, and I am sure they have come to associate words of praise and affirmation with their good performance. But do they know that I take delight in them just because of who they are? I pray so.

Praise, like adoration, requires a personal encounter, but our personal encounters are tainted with our sinful prejudices and expectations. We see others through the eyes of the Evil One rather than through the eyes of God. They must prove themselves worthy of our praise before we will give it. First they must measure up to our standards. So it is with God. There is so much that is wrong in the world that God could and should remedy. The innocent suffer; it rained on my parade; my lost shoe remains lost. *How can I praise a God who lets me down?* we wonder.

Prayer Is Confession

Our encounter with the One who is worthy of our adoration and praise initially makes us aware of our unworthiness. Isaiah's first response to God in the temple was "Woe is me! I am lost, for I am a man of

unclean lips, and I live among a people of unclean lips"
(Isaiah 6:5*a*). The same was true for Peter, who, along
with his fishing companions, had fished all night with no
luck. Jesus told them to go out into the deep water and
throw in their nets. The catch was so great that it began
to sink two boats. Peter responded, "Go away from me,
Lord, for I am a sinful man!" (Luke 5:8*b*).

When we come before the glory of God, our lives are
so illumined that everything secret and hidden is
exposed. Our prideful attempts at pretense are useless.
We cannot help seeing ourselves as we really are, and
the way we really are is sinful.

Before God there is no covering up, but there is
mercy and forgiveness. This is the God whose Word is
Jesus Christ. From his cross forgiveness is pronounced.
A covenant is made: "If we confess our sins, he who is
faithful and just will forgive us our sins and cleanse us
from all unrighteousness" (1 John 1:9).

We are able to confess our sins to God because Jesus
has shown us that God's love for us is greater than our
offense. God's relationship with us will continue. We
will not be abandoned; instead, God wants us to be
released from the power of sin and guilt so that we might
become the persons we were created to be.

James instructs the Christians to whom he writes,
"Therefore confess your sins to one another, and pray for
one another, so that you may be healed" (5:16*a*). That we
are healed by our confession is one of those inexplicable
truths about how we are made and about how God's
Spirit works. Our confession to God and God's forgiveness take on a new quality when we confess to others and
hear their words of absolution on God's behalf.

It seems that we cannot forgive ourselves until we are convinced that God forgives us, and our certainty of God's forgiveness seems to be facilitated by our confession to persons who declare forgiveness in Jesus' name. Listen to the testimony of someone who wrote me following a weekend Emmaus Walk.

> Mike, I cannot tell you in words what it felt like to finally get *all* the truth and pain out in the open. It hurt as bad as anything has ever hurt me. But for once it was a "good hurt." It felt good to finally be able to look you in the eyes. It felt good to have you hold me and tell me that God *had* forgiven me and that I could forgive myself.
>
> It was a miracle for me. I never thought God could reach me. I thought I was too far away.

Our prayer of confession is made to God, but a part of confession's mystery is that it seems it should be made to our sisters and brothers in Christ as well. In a sense, our prayer of confession arises from our solidarity with others. "Since all have sinned and fall short of the glory of God" (Romans 3:23), sin is a corporate matter as well as an individual one.

Our prideful self-justification, however, undermines our solidarity with other sinners. We see so clearly the sins of others while we are blind to our own. Even when we do see our own sins, we rarely perceive them to be as bad as the sins that others have committed. *Surely God grades on the curve!* we think. On the curve, it is every man for himself and every woman for herself. When this happens, we no longer are united by our commonality; we are divided by our competitiveness.

I find myself uniting with those who will aid me in my efforts to prove myself better than my closest competitors; but when they are no longer useful to me, our relationship is terminated. What appears to be solidarity is only expediency and exploitation.

Rarely are we as innocent as we'd like to think. Many sins—such as the "isms" of racism, sexism, ageism, and nationalism—have become so natural for us that we are unaware of them. We sin by our complicity and silence just as we do by our overt participation. What is most important is not that we keep a black mark off our permanent records, but that we be liberated from all that stands in the way of our receiving the freedom and love that are ours through God's mercy.

Confession requires brutal honesty. With our confession, we own up to the sins that God is already aware of but that we have denied. As painful as owning up is, it is a means of grace. The way is now paved for God's salvation. The obstacles to God's healing and empowerment are removed.

Prayer Is Intercession

In his *Genesee Diary*, Henri Nouwen writes:

Often I have said to people, "I will pray for you," but how often did I really enter into the full reality of what that means? . . . Compassion lies at the heart of our prayer for our fellow human beings. When I pray for the world, I become the world, when I pray for the endless needs of the millions, my soul expands and wants to embrace them all and bring them into the presence of God. But in the midst of that experience I realize that compassion is not mine but God's gift to me. I cannot embrace the world, but God can. I cannot pray, but God can pray in me. When God became as we are, that is, when God allowed all of us to enter into the intimacy of the divine life, it became possible for us to share in God's infinite compassion. In praying for others, I lose myself and become the other, only to be found by the divine love which holds the whole of humanity in a compassionate embrace. (Robert Durback, ed., *Seeds of Hope: A Henri Nouwen Reader* [New York: Bantam Books, 1989], pp. 72-73.)

Intercessory prayer is natural for the one who has been made one with humanity through oneness with God. According to Nouwen, through God's intimacy with us in Jesus, we are made to share the virtues of God's life, including compassion. We care as God cares. Therefore, we speak to God the needs of others as if they were our own.

Fred Craddock observed that we'd go crazy hearing the grass grow and listening to leaky faucets if we were not selective about what we attend to. Are we to be concerned about all the world's needs and suffering? If so, how can that be?

I believe the Holy Spirit guides our attentiveness. Some needs will tug at us more than others. Still, through our prayers we can express compassion even for those we are not able to respond to concretely. Except for those of us with Superman or Wonderwoman complexes, however, our sin is not being concerned about too many people, but being concerned about too few. We are masters of rationalization. How quickly our sense of solidarity with the suffering evaporates.

In his article "Killing and Starving to Death" in Moore and Brader's *Philosophy: The Power of Ideas,* James Rachels addresses our rationalizations for not responding in some way to the people around the world who are suffering from malnutrition and starvation. While he does not equate letting people die with murder, he wants us to see that we are guiltier of neglecting the hungry than we assume. He points this out imaginatively by describing an adult man in a room with a child who is obviously starving (hollow eyes, bloated stomach, listless appearance, and so forth). Then he asks what we would think of the man if he were eating a sack lunch and reading a newspaper while ignoring the dying child. If he did not offer the child food or take the child to a hospital for medical attention, we'd think him an immoral monster.

Rachels asks, "What difference does it really make if the starving child is in another room or in another city or across the ocean?" The location of starving people makes a difference to us psychologically, but does it make a difference to us morally? Those whom we can see are more real than those who are far away, but is distance anything more than a convenient means for rationalizing our sense of solidarity and, thus, our responsibility?

Another way we rationalize our detachment is our use of numbers. What difference will feeding this one child make, we ask, when there are millions more who are hungry? Why should I feel guilty for not doing anything when there are so many others who could help but aren't? In fact, many are more affluent than I am.

Ironically, we excuse our lack of solidarity with the starving by appealing to our solidarity with those who are doing nothing. We are selective with our sense of solidarity.

Rachels illustrates how difficult intercessory prayer is for us. Unless we are in communion with God, we are more inclined to perceive ourselves separated from others than joined to them. Without an intimacy with God that is nurtured through prayer, we avoid the suffering of others rather than identify with it.

Interestingly, when we identify with the suffering of others, our prayers of intercession become prayers of confession—for how could we not have identified with their suffering all along, and how could we allow ourselves even to contribute to it? Intercession makes us ripe for confession. Solidarity with others—as well as with Creation—inspires us to both kinds of prayer.

Prayer Is Petition

Whereas intercessory prayer is prayer for others, prayers of petition are prayers for ourselves. But how can we pray for ourselves without sounding petty and selfish? Are we to pray for some of our needs but not for others? Am I to pray for help when I prepare and deliver a talk to the junior high Sunday school class but not when I come to bat in the bottom of the ninth inning with two outs, the bases loaded, and my team behind by one run?

As we mature in Christ, our wants change because we come to value things differently. It's not that we don't believe we're in need of help when we come to bat in a critical game situation, it's simply that we have come to see that athletic competition has its place—and it lies in fellowship and recreation, not in winning or losing. To paraphrase Jesus, we have learned that we can win every game and still lose our soul. As we mature in Christ, our prayers of petition arise from our wanting what God wants. Our prayers are no longer self-centered but Christ-centered.

The truth of the matter is that we do not always know what to pray for. My hunch is that in our independent, do-it-yourself, pull-yourself-up-by-your-bootstraps culture, it is better to err on the side of asking for the wrong things than not asking for anything at all. Not to pray for ourselves may indicate self-deprecation or self-sufficiency. As we pray that God's will be done on earth as in heaven, we must trust God to sort out what we are not yet able to sort out in terms of real, false, and imagined needs.

Some of us want God to do it all and leave us out of it. Many of us, however, have learned the lessons of independence and self-sufficiency too well. We believe that it is better to give than to receive. Therefore, we find it almost impossible to ask God for help. Prayers of petition are hard for us.

Prayer Is Thanksgiving

Rejoice always, pray without ceasing, give thanks in all circumstances; for this is the will of God in Christ Jesus for you. (1 Thessalonians 5:16-18)

Do not worry about anything, but in everything by prayer and supplication with thanksgiving let your requests be made known to God. (Philippians 4:6)

Whereas prayers of adoration and praise focus on God's being, on who God is, prayers of thanksgiving give thanks to God for what God has done. As with the other kinds of prayer, thanksgiving goes against the grain. Unlike Paul, who professed to have learned to be content with whatever he had (Philippians 4:11) and thus could advise the Christians at Thessalonica to give thanks in all circumstances, we find it difficult. We are prone to be more cognizant of what we lack than of what we have.

Advertising and the belief that happiness comes through more and more things have made us chronically discontent with what we have, no matter what it is or how much it is. When we hear a sermon on the ten lepers and Jesus' question, "Where are the nine?" on Thanksgiving Sunday we have a pretty good idea of the answer. We are among those who fail to return to Jesus and give thanks for what he has given. How can we be thankful when there are still some things we lack?

Only by God's grace can we be freed from our wants and perceived needs so that we can be grateful for our abundance. It is an abundance determined not only by counting our blessings. If we are not careful, we will revert to what is basically a limited and selfish perspective. What sustains our personal lives and makes us blessed is of relative importance when compared to what God has done for us to save us from the Evil One for the kingdom of heaven.

We are familiar with Holy Communion, the Lord's Supper. A less familiar name is Eucharist, which comes from the Greek word meaning "thanksgiving." At the center of the Communion liturgy is the prayer "The

Great Thanksgiving." This prayer tells the story of God's plan of salvation. One of the reasons an ordained clergyperson traditionally has presided at the Table is that the church has wanted to be sure that the story is told correctly. "The Great Thanksgiving" begins with Creation, tells of the Fall, and describes how God has sought communion with humankind. The story culminates with how God sent his own Son to speak and live his Word. On the night he was betrayed, Jesus gave his disciples the bread and cup saying, "This is my body and my blood, my life, given for you. Whenever you eat and drink, do it in remembrance of me."

This is our sacrifice of praise and thanksgiving—for what of any value do we have to offer God unless it be what God first has given to us? Our offering is to receive what is given and be thankful. Who could ask for anything more? We do all the time. Prayers of thanksgiving are difficult for us.

Corporate Worship as Prayer

Adoration, praise, confession, intercession, petition, and thanksgiving are elements usually found in our corporate worship services. Corporate worship, then, is an expression of our life of prayer during the week. It also serves as a model for us to follow during the week.

Even preaching is a form of prayer. The purpose of preaching is to assist in keeping the conversation going between God and God's people. On the one hand, the preacher helps the people recognize God's voice and understand the implications of what God is saying. The preacher receives God's Word and proclaims it. On the other hand, the preacher helps God's people listen to themselves and articulate their ongoing efforts to allow God's Word to shape their being and doing.

The sermon, then, is akin to pastoral prayer. It is a response to a God who has spoken. The preacher dares to speak on God's behalf and accepts the challenge of speaking on behalf of the people—of knowing human nature well enough to give voice to the soul's deepest needs. The preacher embodies the dialogue between God and God's people. In and through the preacher the dialogue is facilitated. The preacher stands as an intermediary who hears and helps others to hear; who speaks and helps other to make God's language, God's logic, their own.

Disciplines for Prayer

When persons come to me for counseling they often say, "I don't know where to begin." Then they give a deep sigh which says their story is so heavy that it seems to have no beginning or end. My response is, "Just jump in anywhere. Beginning is what is important."

The same is true for prayer. Our conversation with one another—at least our conversation that leads to intimacy—does not conform to some prescribed formula. We just "jump in," and then our vulnerability, honesty, openness, risk, and love take over from there. We cannot predict what will happen. We may not know exactly what we will say, much less how it will be received.

Many believe that in order to pray we must be verbally eloquent or spiritually pure. It doesn't take much for us to talk ourselves out of praying; almost any excuse will do. Therefore, the key is to begin—and we can begin simply.

Practicing the Presence of God

A seventeenth-century monk named Brother Lawrence learned to "practice the presence of God" while he was working in the kitchen of his monastery. His example reminds us that we can "pray without ceasing" in all circumstances—even while we are on K.P.! Our conversation with God continues all the time if we are aware of God's presence.

But being aware of God's presence all the time is not easy. Much of our time is described in the New Testament as *chronos* time. This is the time we "kill" because it is barren of meaning and full of burden and boredom. *Chronos* time is not like *kairos* time, or prayerful time, which is pregnant with God. Living in *kairos* time, we lean into the future expectantly on the alert for God's surprises. Life lived in *kairos* time is abundant and eternal.

Living in *kairos* time requires discipline. We generally are preoccupied with concerns about our personal welfare and those close to us. We do not practice the presence of God as much as we practice the presence of our self-centered agendas, which usually are responses to our anxiety, greed, and fear. We must make a willful commitment to practice the presence of God.

One of the ways to practice the presence of God is what Episcopal priest Ron Delbene refers to as the *breath prayer*—a short prayer that we pray periodically throughout the day and that becomes as natural to us as breathing. We begin the prayer with the name we generally use to address God. For you it may be Almighty God, Father, Mother, Lord, Jesus, or Spirit.

Then, as we imagine the Holy One approaching us, we hear the questions, What can I do for you? What is your need? Our response is to be brief and is to entail the essence of what we need from God.

Thus, your breath prayer might be, "Lord, give me your peace," or "Jesus, heal me of my guilt." I've found the petition of the psalmist—although longer than Delbene recommends—to be an appropriate breath prayer for myself: O God, "create in me a clean heart . . . and put a new and right spirit within me" (51:10). The *Kyrie Eleison* of the church's liturgical tradition is another example: "Lord, have mercy upon us; Christ, have mercy upon us; Lord, have mercy upon us."

While waiting at the stoplight, standing in line at the grocery store, or lying in bed before falling sleep or after turning the alarm off, we pray a breath prayer and come into the presence of a God who has been present all along and has been waiting for our acknowledgment. We admit our dependence on God and our trust in God's love for us.

Praying the Scriptures

Because prayer is conversation with God and includes our listening as well as our speaking, the discipline of praying the Scriptures is a helpful way to come into the presence of God and to hear God's voice. Praying the Scriptures, or some other spiritual literature, focuses our mind and heart in such a way as to place us in a posture for hearing what God is saying through the written word.

The object is not to impose our own interpretations upon the text but to be open to hearing what we have not heard before or what we have forgotten and to submit ourselves to the passage and humbly receive what it will give. Because God is the giver and God gives as God will, we are to be patient and tolerant of silence when we pray the Scriptures. On occasion we may hear nothing. In that case, we resist reading something into the text just to have something "to take home" for our efforts. Silence may be what God knows we need to "hear" at the moment.

The key is not to dissect and analyze a Scripture passage but to become one with it. We can do this imaginatively through the senses that are stimulated by the passage's setting. We also can pick a character or characters in the passage through which to experience what is taking place. By moving from character to character, we gain the advantage of multiple perspectives. Then we ask ourselves, What word or act is heard or seen that runs contrary to the normal way life works and is expected to work? Is this a word from the Lord?

Whether we are prayerfully reading the Scriptures or using some other form of listening prayer, we must be careful to "check out" what we believe to be a word from the Lord. Past experience, Christian tradition, and other Christians whose counsel is valued are ways to assess what we have heard to be sure it is not the voice of the Evil One or our own wishful thinking.

Praying Through Writing

Even for those who find writing a natural form of self-expression, it remains a demanding discipline. In my experience, writing is a means God uses for creating order in the chaos of our inner lives and all that resides in them. Writing can be the occasion for discovering meaning in what often "feels" meaningless. It "gets out on the table" and makes objective what has been overwhelmingly subjective. My inner "mess" of jumbled and hostile forces makes me its victim and controls me in ways of which I am unconscious. Writing helps me to become clear about what the "mess" really is.

In his book *The Living Reminder*, Henri Nouwen describes insightfully the phenomenon of absence. He quotes Jesus' words to his disciples before his death: "Nevertheless I tell you the truth: it is to your advantage that I go away, for if I do not go away, the Helper will not come to you; but if I go, I will send him to you" (John 16:7). Earlier Jesus had said, "But the Helper, the Holy Spirit, whom the Father will send in my name, will teach you everything, and remind you of all that I have said to you" (14:26). With the help of the Holy Spirit, the disciples would come to know and appreciate Jesus more after he was gone than while he was with them.

My experience, and I suspect yours also, confirms Nouwen's insight that leaving and being absent can be as beneficial as arriving and being present. This is contrary to popular wisdom. "Getting away" from a situation often gives me a new and beneficial perspective that probably would not have come had I remained in the situation. Sometimes the farther we are from something the better we are able to see it.

Writing is a way of gaining distance while we remain geographically near. Reflection takes us out of the immediacy of our experience and permits us to "step back" for a look from a different vantage point. For this reason, many have found *journaling* to be a beneficial discipline in their ongoing conversation with God.

As I write I am aware that God is listening in. In fact, I now write as though I'm writing to God. When I read what I have written, I become aware that the One to whom I am writing is present implicitly in the content of what I'm writing. In other words, my words talk back to me.

What is true for the breath prayer is also true for journaling: simply begin and begin simply. You don't have to write a book each time you sit down! Nor do you have to write as though you were going to be published. What you write is private. It is between you and God. You don't have to write complete sentences or to punctuate correctly. An entry may be no more than a few phrases or sentences.

The important thing is to back away with God in order to see what is going on in your life and to listen for God's Spirit which seeks to "teach you everything." By being "absent" from a situation, you are placed in a position to see and hear something new. You may see yourself as others—and God—see you. Writing about a troubling incident and your part in it may produce the reaction, "I can't believe I did that! This is not the kind of person I want to be. I have let my Lord down. I must go, apologize, and make amends."

Journaling may precipitate confession and repentance. It may also be a source of inspiration and hope. As we write, this retrospective vantage point enables us to see how God has been involved with us and how we have been oblivious to it. We have thought we were alone and even abandoned, but now we can see how God has been with us all along. Having gained appreciation for how God has been with us, we now have a sense of direction for where God is leading us. We hear a call that provides us orientation and focuses our energies.

Journaling can be a means for God to help us find ourselves when we are lost. It can remind us of whose we are and who we are. It can help us center our fragmented and frantic lives in God.

So buy a notebook or composition book and spend time each day reflecting on what is going on in your life. (Remember this is a discipline, so you may not write *every* day at first.) Take your spiritual pulse. Write God a letter. You may want to answer the following questions:

For what or whom are you grateful?
How has your life been blessed?
Who or what has been a means of grace for you?
What is burdening you?
What are you angry about?
What is making you fearful?
What is the source of your guilt?
Who has hurt you?
What are you uncertain about?
What regrets do you have?
Who needs you to reach out to them?
Is God calling you to be faithful to a former ministry?
Is God calling you into something new?
Are those closest to you needing something from you that you've been unaware of?
What word from God have you heard as a result of prayerfully reading the Scriptures? How does God want you to apply this word to your life?

Letter writing can be another aid to prayer. Distance from the ones to whom we are writing can help us to see them in a way that is not possible when we are with them. Our absence enables us to be present to them in words that we might never be able to say to them face-to-face. Honesty and vulnerability may be expressed in the letter which prepares the way for the divine gift of intimacy. We are able to say some things that need to be said and to hear some things that need to be heard.

In our journaling we may be more conscious of God because we understand that what we write is addressed to God. Yet even in our letters that are addressed to others, God is present, overhearing our conversation and wanting to bless it with grace. God wants our communication to prepare the way for holy communion with God and others.

A final way writing can be an aid to prayer is through imaginative writing. I'll say more about imagination later, but for the present let me suggest that you imagine what God would write to you. Pretend you are God's scribe and you are writing a letter that God is dictating. The letter is to you. What do you think God would want to say to you right now? This exercise can be an effective stimulus for getting the conversation going if you have reached a place in your prayer life where nothing seems to be "getting through."

Guided Meditation

As Peter seeks to interpret the manifestations of the Holy Spirit on the day of Pentecost, he draws on the prophet Joel: "In the last days it will be, God declares, that I will pour out my Spirit upon all flesh, and your sons and your daughters shall prophesy, and your young men shall see visions, and your old men shall dream dreams" (Acts 2:17). The Spirit's presence enables persons to see beyond the immediate present. The Spirit stirs the various levels of human consciousness. Our intimacy with God entails our whole being. It includes our subconscious and our imagination.

Here is an example of a guided meditation. Persons are asked to get into a comfortable position and prepare to listen attentively to God. They are asked to place their hands "palms up" on their knees and to fill their palms with those things that are bothering them—such as anger at someone who has been hurtful, concern for a friend, conflict with a relative, worry about school or job performance. Imagining that God has come to them, they are to turn their palms down and watch God collecting those things that have been dropped. Then they are to turn their palms up again and to imagine God placing in their hands what they need. (Based on *Journey Into Faith: A Confirmation Resource for Junior Highs, Leader's Guide* [Nashville: Graded Press, 1984], p. 58.)

This guided meditation functions much as the letter-from-God exercise; it involves our whole selves in the conversation with God. We are enabled to see that God loves us and, therefore, comes to us. God seeks intimacy with us through interaction with us.

Flora Slosson Wuellner believes guided meditation can be a means for God to heal our inner wounds. In her book *Prayer, Stress, and Our Inner Wounds* (Nashville: The Upper Room, 1985), she describes what she calls "Prayer for the Inner Child":

> Picture Jesus Christ (in whatever form the love of God through Christ best comes to you) entering the room and filling it with warmth and comfort. He who said, "Let the children come to me" (Luke 18:16), now tenderly calls forth your own most deeply wounded, problematic self.
>
> The one you have hidden, the one you have hated, the one within who feels the weakest, the ugliest, the most vulnerable, the most shameful, the frightening or the most frightened comes forward—like a hurt child. . . . Together, you and Jesus look on it compassionately. Look at the expression in its face, and listen to what it is trying to say in its own words. You need not fear it, because the love of God in Jesus is with you.
>
> Embrace your "child" if you can, but do not force yourself to do this if you don't want to touch it. Later this reluctance will also be healed. . . . Now release your inner child to Jesus' healing hands. . . . Ask Jesus to come to you both, putting his arms around both you and the inner child. But if you can, imagine Jesus taking your inner child fully into his hands and arms, into the light, into the central heart of love, and holding it there.
>
> Sit quietly, giving thanks that this deep, central, hurting part of yourself is now being deeply held, comforted, healed, restored slowly to its original beauty and unique creativity.

Guided meditations, like this one, invite us to believe that God wants what we know we so desperately need. God wants our wounded "inner children" to be healed.

How that healing will come we cannot dictate. Our belief, however, is that God will provide grace sufficient for the need, if we are receptive to it.

Praying with Others

A spiritual hunger is being manifested in our nation and around the world. One of the ways this hunger is being addressed is through small groups of Christians who pray together and share their needs.

To ask someone to pray for a specific need can be a fearful experience. To drop your guard and allow yourself to be exposed to the judgment of others entails risk. We don't want others to know how weak we are, for they may take advantage of us. We don't want them to know how we have failed, for they may condemn us. We don't want them to know our secret feelings and impulses, for they may humiliate us. But it is both evidence of grace and a means of grace to pray with someone. Praying together celebrates our unity in the Body of Christ and nurtures that unity further.

Emphasis on small groups appears to be a common trait of vital and growing churches. These groups take a variety of forms. Among them are Covenant Discipleship groups, Cursillo and Emmaus Walk reunion groups, combination Bible study and prayer groups, and short-term topical study groups. The "group" may consist of only two people—you and a "spiritual friend" who agrees to be honest and vulnerable with you in the name of Jesus.

Jesus promised to be with those who gather in his name and to respond to the prayers of the faithful when they agree: "Again, truly I tell you, if two of you agree on earth about anything you ask, it will be done for you by my Father in heaven. For where two or three are gathered in my name, I am there among them" (Matthew 18:19-20). I do not understand fully this promise of Jesus to do what any two of his disciples agree upon. Perhaps this agreement is intended to serve as a means for checking the disciples' prayer requests to determine—to the degree that it is humanly possible—whether they are God's will or merely our self-centered human desires. Surely we do not believe that if two persons agree to ask for a winning lottery ticket, God will give it.

One small group that is easy to overlook is the family. Ironically, the family, which is supposed to be the most intimate of relationships, is often the last place where persons want to be honest and vulnerable in prayer. Sharing of this kind does not come easy in any context; it requires our acceptance of grace, which frees us to be known by others without defensiveness and to know others without judgment.

Therefore, families that pray together must work at it. It takes practice. The goal is that family prayer becomes a habit, but not the kind of habit that is done unconsciously. The habitual character of family prayer entails a growing dedication by each of the family members to the discipline of honest and vulnerable conversation in the name and Spirit of Jesus.

A place to begin is the dinner table, though this last vestige of the family assembly is being threatened by the microwave and fast food restaurant. If your family still eats a common meal together, it might be useful for each person to share before the blessing what he or she is thankful for and what he or she needs or is concerned about. The person chosen to pray then could include these expressions of thanksgiving, petition, confession, and intercession in the prayer so that it becomes the prayer of the entire family.

By praying together, family members may become spiritually related. Jesus observed this is the kind of relatedness that matters most: "For whoever does this will of my Father in heaven is my brother and sister and mother" (Matthew 12:5). In our culture's preoccupation with the demise of the nuclear family, we are prone to forget that our families are to be viewed as means to the fulfillment of God's purposes rather than as ends in themselves.

Corporate Intercessory Prayer

Dr. Ted Jennings has observed that the pastoral prayer in corporate worship is of crucial importance because it teaches the congregation how to pray. If the prayer consists of flowery speech but empty words, the congregation will dismiss prayer as inconsequential. If the prayer is self-centered and its horizons are narrow, the congregation's parochialism will be reinforced. If the prayer never addresses what is controversial or asks for what everyone needs but is afraid to acknowledge, the congregation will view prayer as powerless.

In some traditions the pastor is referred to as the parson, the person. Through this person we experience Christ's person. Through this person we see and hear one who is intimate with Christ. Through this person we learn what God's person cares about and wants.

This means the one who prays the pastoral prayer in worship dares to see what many would rather hide their eyes from. It means that he or she will dare to say what many are afraid to say. It means that the truth of our confusion and ambivalence will be confessed. It means that prayers will be voiced for the enemy and for others whom many would rather not pray for. The pastoral prayer tells a lot about the pastor who prays it, the people on whose behalf it is prayed, the God to whom it is prayed, and the relationship they all share.

As worship becomes decreasingly clergy-centered, the role of the laity becomes more prominent. An example is the intercessory prayer. The clergyperson may lead it, but there are pauses that invite members of the congregation to voice their personal concerns and concerns for others. Following the voiced thanksgiving, confession, petition, or intercession, the congregation makes the prayer its own with words such as, "Hear our prayer, O Lord," or "Lord, in your mercy, hear our prayer."

Congregations that pray together are glued together by the Spirit of Christ and experience the communion that results when people speak the same holy language. It is a language grounded in love.

A Word About Solitude

One cannot address the disciplines of prayer without speaking of solitude. Much has been said and written about solitude, but it can never be too much. In our present culture, solitude is anathema. Even those of us who are introverts feel that our time alone must be filled with activity and productivity. We are "doing" people. Our identity and self-esteem come from what we do. It is so very hard for us to "be."

Speaking for God, the psalmist says, "Be still, and know that I am God!" (46:10). It may well be that one of the manifestations of our desire to be like God is our nonstop activity. Our sabbaths are not days of rest but days full of different activities. On our vacations we vacate—we empty—our lives of one thing only to fill them with something else.

"Be still, and know that I am God!" I am recommending what I am still in the early stages of learning—that doing nothing sometimes may be the most worthwhile thing for me to do (or is it not to do?). I seem to come closest to being still when I am walking alone in a state park about an hour from where I live and work. I have to physically displace myself to center on God and be attentive. Walking is a way of keeping my body busy so that my soul may listen. Someday maybe my body will be able to be still and listen, too.

Transformed by Prayer

Prayer changes things. It also changes those who pray. It is not possible to explain precisely how the changes occur or what changes can be predicted. Prayer, like all conversation and communication, affects both the speaker and hearer in ways that are not entirely under the control of either. In other words, because prayer is conversation with God, it remains a mystery.

Nevertheless, there are some qualities of character and behavior that are common to those who are attentive to God, for this God to whom we pray is the God revealed in Jesus Christ. This God to whom we pray is the God who remains active in the world through the power of the Holy Spirit. The Bible and tradition give testimony to how Jesus lived and to what the Holy Spirit is "up to."

Therefore, once we have heard God's Word, who we are and how we respond take on a distinctive character. This is true for individuals and for the church. The following description of the character of those who are prayerful is just a beginning. You will be able to add to it as you observe those who pray and as you yourself are prayerful.

The Prayerful Are Centered

In a world where the Evil One's governance has not been completely replaced by the kingdom of heaven, we are constantly tempted to be discontent with who we are and what we have. We spend our lives trying to be someone other than who we are. Who we are is not good enough. Consciously or unconsciously, therefore, we spend our lives trying to be like God, whom we have defined as self-sufficient, all-knowing, controlling, invincible, and "above it all."

The logic or reasoning that rules this kind of life compels us to do those things that will prove we are somebody special in the eyes of others. Because we take our cue from the mirror image we see of ourselves in others' eyes, it is crucial that we get them to think of us as we want to think of ourselves.

We become proficient false self-advertisers. What people see is not who we are. We lie, deceive, hide, cover up, and manipulate, but we cannot escape that sense from deep within our being that this dishonesty is wrong. Moreover, we are forever afraid of being found out—of the truth about us becoming known. As long as we can keep others from knowing the truth about us, we won't have to accept it ourselves.

Prayerful persons have heard the truth about themselves; it comes from the Word of God. In Jesus we have been told that we are God's own daughters and sons. Whatever is not right about us is forgiven. God's love for us seeks reconciliation, not condemnation. God has declared us righteous, for God can see in us more than we can see in ourselves. God can see the holy image in us that was placed there at our creation. Becoming who God created us to be is what we now live for. We live to be like God, but we know that being holy entails love rather than knowledge, control, or invincibility.

Because we are centered in God, God's Word determines our identity and value rather than the words of the Evil One and his spokespersons. We no longer frantically seek to prove we are worthy of being loved. God loves us, and this is the love that matters. We are not anxious about who we have not yet become, for we know that by God's grace and in God's time we will become who we are meant to be. We don't *have* to be someone other than who we are; we *want* to be. We want to give glory to the One who created us, who loved us despite our sin, and who now seeks to recreate us and free us from the power of sin and death.

As a result of God's freeing love, prayerful persons want what God wants, even if it means sacrificing their own wants or having to admit that their own wants are unholy. They pray to see life as God sees it. They ask God for the same thing Solomon asked for when he became king.

When God appeared to Solomon in a dream, God told him, "Ask what I should give you" (1 Kings 3:5). Solomon replied, "Give your servant . . . an understanding mind to govern your people, able to discern between good and evil" (verse 9). Solomon wanted what God wanted. Some have said that the "understanding mind" he asked for might be better translated as a "seeing heart." Freed from our bondage to sin—now God-centered rather than self-centered—we want to see life from God's vantage point. Prayer positions us at God's vantage point.

Just as individuals receive their identity by being centered in God, so also do churches. Churches, like individuals, can exhaust themselves trying to be what they are not in order to prove to the culture that they serve a worthwhile function.

The church is tempted by words other than God's Word to be something other than what Christ called it to be. Many churches now advertise themselves as "full-service" churches. Everything anyone could want is provided under one roof. The result is that sometimes it's hard to tell a church from a civic club, a fitness center, a day-care center, a social service agency, a department store, or a gambling casino.

Believing that it has nothing of enduring value to offer the world, the church has chosen to sell itself in the marketplace. It now competes for people's time, energy, and financial resources. As Peter Berger explains in his book *The Sacred Canopy,* the church, which is dependent upon people's loyalty for its sense of worth as well as its institutional survival, seeks to discover what the people want so that it may give it to them. It conforms to the world, rather than inviting the world to conform to it.

In perceiving itself as a marketable commodity, has the church compromised itself? In seeking to gain the whole world, is the church in risk of losing its own soul? Prayer helps churches answer these questions. Prayer keeps churches centered in God's Word.

What does a prayer-centered church look like? A prayer-centered church looks like Jesus. It is obedient to God's love. Through it the world experiences God's logic of self-giving and self-sacrifice. It names the world's demons and seeks the world's release from the evil powers and principalities. It teaches the world a new language—God's language. This language calls into being God's reign, the kingdom of heaven.

A prayer-centered church is available to God. It listens to God's Word and allows God's Word to determine who it is and what it does. While it practices long-range planning, it remains ever open to altering its "best laid" plans.

A prayer-centered church is on guard, lest it be seduced by the world's bottom-line criteria for measuring success. It is willing to be a servant to "the least of these." It has heard God's Word and believes that life is to be received not in self-preoccupation but in self-denial. Therefore, it genuinely seeks to love those within and outside its membership. It desires the realization of that oneness by which the world will come to know the God of Jesus Christ.

The Prayerful Are Patient and Persevering

Prayerful persons are not easily discouraged. Seeing things from God's vantage point enables them to see the big picture. What they are a part of matters more than their personal self-gratification. Consequently, they do not take personally others' resistance to or rejection of the good news of God's salvation. Prayer strengthens their faith in the coming of the kingdom of heaven. They are content to be faithful in the present and to entrust the future to God.

Because prayerful persons seek to be faithful rather than successful, they can take risks. They can fail without being destroyed or becoming disillusioned. They can dream God's dreams and act on them without any guarantee that those dreams will be realized.

I once served as chairperson of the board of directors of an ecumenical agency for emergency relief in a local community. The executive director of the agency was named Mary. "Executive director" doesn't fit Mary; "servant" does. I recall the winter night Mary called me. "Mike," she said, "the temperature's dropping, and the police are finding men sleeping outside in garbage dumpsters, bushes, and alleys around the city. I'm afraid someone is going to die in this cold. I'm going to call some of the churches and see if they'll let these people sleep in their buildings until the weather warms up."

Mary did not stop there. At the next board meeting she reported: "God has laid on my heart the plight of these homeless men in our city. I've talked with a man who owns an abandoned church building just down the street. I think we can buy it and fix it up as a dormitory for men to stay in while they get back on their feet. The man wants $28,000, but I think he'll take $16,500."

"Mary," I replied, "now let's be practical. We're hardly meeting our budget now. Where do you think we're going to get $16,500 to purchase the building and another $1,500 to renovate it? I think your dreams have gone too far this time."

In her soft-spoken manner, Mary responded, "The

Lord will provide if this is something God wants us to do and if we are faithful to try." Mary then asked the board for permission to attempt to raise the money herself. We said, "Sure, but don't expect much help from us."

The deadline that had been set for raising the money was approaching. Mary had managed to collect about $10,000. It looked like her dream would have to be forsaken.

The pastor of a local church dropped by Mary's office one day. He told her about a man in his church who wanted to donate some money to help needy persons in the city. The man had asked the pastor for advice on where the money should go, and the pastor had affirmed the work that Mary and the agency were doing. So the man had given the pastor a check for $6,500—enough to purchase the building that would become a shelter for homeless men.

Today a city has a ministry to homeless men because a woman would not be discouraged by the doubt of others. Although Mary never said it to me, she could have: "O ye of little faith." Mary taught me a lesson about being patient and persevering. She taught me about the power of listening to the burdens of God communicated to her in prayer and then acting to relieve them. She trusted God's communication with her. Her faith led her to respond to her "call" to raise the necessary money.

The Prayerful Are Discerning

Those who are in conversation with God have ears and eyes that provide a backdrop against which to judge the present situation. Prayerful persons are able to be empathetic with those who are hurting. At the same time, however, they are able to see beyond the hurt to the kingdom of heaven for which Jesus prayed, lived, and died. Prayerful persons know that even though feelings may be justified, acting on them may not be right for those who are committed to the way, truth, and life of Jesus.

Prayerful persons are able to supply at a particular point in time what others are lacking. In a different situation, the shoe may be on the other foot. The one who once was the giver may now be the receiver.

A woman seemed almost shell-shocked as she told her story to the prayer group. She had experienced one loss after another. Her husband had left her for another woman. Her mother had died. Her son had been arrested and put in jail for selling drugs. She had been laid off from her job. She said to the group: "I feel numb. I've lost my faith in God. I'm having trouble seeing any reason to go on living." A member of the group responded: "We'll hold on to you and we'll hold on to your faith until you are able to take it back again. Until then, let our faith carry you."

Sometimes life's circumstances overwhelm us so much that we can't see the light at the end of the tunnel. The darkness is too thick. The only thing that will keep us going is the testimony of those who can see the light shining through the darkness.

I can imagine situations when my feelings would make me want to act in ways contrary to my commitment to the way of Christ. I suspect you can, too. For example, if a drunk driver hit a car my children were riding in and they were killed, I would want to kill the driver. I would want to inflict as much suffering on the driver as he or she had inflicted. In my loss and outrage, I would be tempted to become someone other than the person in Christ whom I know I am. Therefore, I would need those in the Christian community who were not hurting as much as I to share what they had that I, at that time, did not. I would need them to witness to mercy and forgiveness, because I could not.

Prayerful people and churches are called on to do this all the time. Those who hear such a calling know it is a test of their faithfulness to the kingdom of heaven which Jesus revealed in God's will. There are those who, because of their upbringing, are racially prejudiced. Those who believe that God's love transcends race are called to witness to them. There are those who, because of their condemnation of homosexuals, refuse compassion for those with AIDS. Those who have heard God's word of mercy and compassion are called to witness to them.

Prayerful persons and churches believe it is not how we feel that is most important but how we can be faithful through our witness to the reign of God revealed in Jesus Christ.

The Prayerful Are Vital

Prayerful persons and churches are faithful and vital. They are alive because they have the breath of Jesus in them. They are inspired by the Holy Spirit. Their life energy comes not from themselves but from God.

When our life comes from the Holy Spirit, we cannot predict where it will take us. Speaking to Nicodemus about being born anew, Jesus said, "The wind [Spirit] blows where it chooses, and you hear the sound of it, but you do not know where it comes from or where it goes. So it is with everyone who is born of the Spirit" (John 3:8). By being receptive to the unpredictable directions of the Spirit's blowing, the vital Christian and the vital church are open to change. "We've never done it this way before" may be true, but it is not the law—the logic—of those who pray.

Those who have an ongoing conversation with God are likely to hear anything. Everything that is assumed to be eternally "nailed down" is susceptible to being pulled up and undone. Those who have had ears to hear bear testimony.

Noah was told to build an ark on dry land. Abraham and Sarah left their home for a promised land they had never seen. Jonah was told to go to Nineveh—the last place on earth he wanted to go. Joseph intended to break his engagement to Mary because she was pregnant, but he had a dream, heard God's voice, and changed his mind. Peter heard God's word in a dream about clean and unclean animals. For him it was a word telling him that Gentiles were not to be excluded from the church.

Then there was Jesus. Some might protest that I would suggest Jesus listened to God and then changed his mind—for wasn't he so attuned to God that his every thought was God's thought? I believe that Jesus, sharing in our full humanity, had thoughts of his own as we do. He submitted them to God as we do. Jesus' prayer in the Garden of Gethsemane is an example. He prayed for deliverance, but he proceeded to Golgotha.

Consider Jesus' encounter with the Canaanite woman

who pleaded with him on behalf of her daughter who was tormented by a demon (Matthew 15:22ff). At first Jesus did not respond to her at all. Then he said that he was sent only to the lost sheep of the house of Israel. He defended his unresponsiveness by likening it to throwing the children's food to the dogs. The woman replied, "Then just treat me as you would a dog, for dogs are permitted to eat the crumbs from their masters' table." With this, Jesus had a change of mind. Her faith struck a cord within his "seeing heart." He was moved to be God's Word for her and her daughter.

Prayerful persons and prayerful churches have their minds and hearts changed. They want what God wants. They grow in love and become lovers like the One who loves them. This love is eternal; it has no end. It reaches out even to the enemy.

Thus, love's work is never finished. As long as there are persons in need of what God wants for them, there will be something for the church and its members to do; and as long as the church is open to doing what God wants it to do, it will be vital and alive. It makes no difference where it is, how big it is, or how wealthy it is.

The Prayerful Are Hopeful

Prayerful people and prayerful churches do not despair when circumstances overwhelm them. Centered in God, they see from God's vantage point and seek to be faithful, even in the midst of decline and the absence of obvious indicators of success. They do not curse the darkness, because they have learned to see by the light of Christ.

About six years ago a Tuesday afternoon prayer group began to pray for a spiritual revival in their church. Soon a Wednesday night dinner followed by small-group experiences for all ages became a weekly event. About one hundred persons gathered regularly to eat, pray, learn, and love together. Not long after that, persons from the congregation began attending Emmaus Walks, and the youth began attending Chrysalis weekends. An early morning Sunday worship service was added. The informal service included "praise songs," personal testimonies of thanksgiving for God's gifts, voiced intercessory prayer concerns, and weekly Holy Communion. Three Covenant Discipleship groups were started. The church built and paid for a new education building. The church's missional giving and outreach increased. A member of the church became the first member to participate in a Volunteers in Mission project. Others began to witness a new sense of friendliness and caring among the membership.

This small group perceived a need within their church. God gave them grace which enabled them to believe that the Holy Spirit wanted to move in new ways in their congregation. In hope they prayed. The spiritual revival might have happened without the prayers of their small group, for God works in mysterious ways. Still, I believe that their prayers contributed to the realization of what Christ wants for their church.

The Prayerful Follow Jesus

Prayer may be a stationary activity for many. We may pray while we're kneeling, reclining, or sitting. Nevertheless, prayer can be counted on to *move* us.

Because prayer centers us in God, it moves us away from other centers. It moves us against the grain. Prayer moves us to be hopeful, patient, and persevering because it enables us to see things from God's vantage point. It permits our lives to be led in directions we've never gone before. Then we are willing to risk unpopularity and even our lives.

Across the road from the Abbey of Gethsemane at Trappist, Kentucky, there is a path that winds up to the top of a hill. Along the way it follows a brook, crosses the levee of a lake, and offers benches for the tired and meditative. At the end of the path are two statues. The first statue is of Peter, James, and John sleeping. A plaque beside it reads in part:

GARDEN OF GETHSEMANE
IN MEMORY OF JONATHAN M. DANIELS,
EPISCOPALIAN SEMINARIAN
MARTYRED IN ALABAMA, AUGUST 20, 1965

The limestone path continues up the hill to the second sculpture. Jesus is on his knees—his face toward heaven and his hands covering his face.

Jesus prayed in Gethsemane, where he was arrested and then taken to be crucified. "Thy will be done and not mine," he prayed. Jonathan M. Daniels was murdered for following the One who was crucified for living the prayer that God's will might be done on earth as it is in heaven. Jonathan had been helping with voter registration in Alabama when he was arrested along with several blacks. He took a bullet intended for a black woman as they were being let out of jail.

"Prayer will take you someplace," my brother-in-law commented as we discussed the sculptures and the Episcopalian seminarian in whose memory they were given. It took Jesus to Golgotha. It took Jonathan Daniels to Alabama.

Be attentive to God for very long, and the eyes and hands and feet will be as involved as the ears and mouth. Prayer will take you someplace.

I am greatly indebted to my former professor, Theodore W. Jennings, Jr., for his contributions to my theological thoughts about worship and prayer. I recommend two of his books in this area: *Life as Worship: Prayer and Praise in Jesus' Name* (Grand Rapids: Eerdmans, 1982) and *The Liturgy of Liberation: The Confession and Forgiveness of Sins* (Nashville: Abingdon Press, 1988).

If you have not yet discovered Henri Nouwen, you will be delighted when you do. Robert Durback provides a collection of excerpts from several of Nouwen's books and other writings in *Seeds of Hope: A Henri Nouwen Reader* (New York: Bantam Books, 1989).

Another book you may find helpful is Richard Foster's *Celebration of Discipline: The Path to Spiritual Growth* (San Francisco: Harper & Row, 1988). Look particularly at the chapters on "Meditation," "Prayer," "Solitude," "Confession," and "Worship."

In his book *Who Needs God?* (New York: Summit Books, 1989), Harold Kushner describes insightfully the cultural milieu in which we pray. Chapter 7 is entitled "Can Modern People Pray?"

John B. Cobb, Jr., explores intercessory prayer in *Praying for Jennifer: An Exploration of Intercessory Prayer in Story Form* (Nashville: The Upper Room, 1985). Metropolitan Anthony Bloom writes from a Russian Orthodox perspective in *Living Prayer* (Springfield, Ill.: Templegate, 1975). Douglas V. Steere speaks from a Quaker point of view in *Dimensions of Prayer* (Women's Division, General Board of Global Ministries, The United Methodist Church, 1962).

For those interested in other guided meditations, be sure to secure a copy of Flora Slosson Wuellner's *Prayer, Stress, and Our Inner Wounds* (Nashville: The Upper Room, 1985). The book is full of what she calls *imagery prayers.*

If you're interested in journaling, you may find Anne Broyle's *Journaling: A Spirit Journey* (Nashville: The Upper Room: 1988) helpful. I've found that The Upper Room's annual *Journeying Through the Days: A Calendar/Journal for Personal Reflection* provides the incentive I need to maintain my journaling through those hectic periods when solitude gets squeezed out by the demands of life and ministry. In this annually published book, a verse of Scripture from each week's lectionary readings is the setting for a block of "blank space" for recording reflections. The photographs and their accompanying quotations are worth the price of the book.

Ron Delbene, along with Mary and Herb Montgomery, has written several helpful books, including *Into the Light: A Simple Way to Pray with the Sick and Dying* (Nashville: The Upper Room, 1988).

Maxie Dunnam has written several workbooks for small groups interested in prayer and the spiritual life. The series, published by The Upper Room, now includes these titles: *The Workbook of Living Prayer* (1974), *The Workbook of Intercessory Prayer* (1979), *The Workbook on Spiritual Disciplines* (1984), *The Workbook on Becoming Alive in Christ* (1986), and *The Workbook on Coping as Christians* (1988).